Covid-19 Back to School Guide

for

Parents and Students

William A. Haseltine PhD

Thank you for buying the *Covid Back To School Guide*, the companion book to our *Family Guide to Covid*. Like the *Family Guide*, this *Back To School* book is a living book. As our understanding of the disease and the nature of the outbreak changes, so will the contents of this book.

As the owner of this book, you now have a permanent pass to every edition to come.

Visit www.accessh.org/covidfamilyguide
Click on the Back To School Guide
And enter the password: BackToSchool

You'll be taken to a special section of our website where you can download the most up to date version.

I hope you find this book useful as you decide whether a return to school is right for you and your family.

Sincerely,
Dr. Bill

CONTENTS

Foreword 1

Chapter 1: A Critical Need to Reopen Schools 10

Chapter 2: Know Your Community 16

Chapter 3: Know Your Risk 36

Chapter 4: Know Your School 54

Chapter 5: Remote Learning and Other
   Opportunities To Learn 74

Chapter 6: Personal Strategies 83

Epilogue.. 88

Acknowledgements 120

Appendix... 122

Foreword

Over the past few weeks and months, I have had countless conversations with family and friends who are struggling with a heartbreaking question: should I send my child back to school in the midst of the Covid pandemic or should I risk my job and my family's income to keep them home and safe? Unfortunately, parents and students are essentially alone in making this life and death decision, with little guidance being offered by government leaders and little assurance that decisions on reopening schools are grounded in public health and not politics.

This book is for every parent and student struggling with the question of whether to return to school. In the following chapters, I will walk you through the questions you should be asking yourselves, your school administrators, and your local leaders before deciding whether to return to the classroom. I will also talk about the level of leadership, commitment, and investment you should expect from your government and school boards to ensure all the measures that will protect our students are in place by the fall.

These are issues dear to my heart. While I am a scientist by training and have spent a lifetime studying infectious diseases, I am first and foremost a father and grandfather. My children and grandchildren are struggling with the same challenges you are struggling with today.

When they ask me what I think about heading back to school, I give them one of two answers — the short version and the long version. The long version is what I explore in the subsequent chapters of this book. The short version is this: there are three things that everyone must know *with certainty* before being able to make a decision about returning to school:

First, you need to know the risk of infection in your community — whether Covid cases are on the rise or not.

Second, you need to know your family's personal risk — whether you, your immediate family or your close circle of loved ones are at risk of severe illness from a Covid infection.

Third, you need to know what your school is going to do to keep students and staff safe. The hard truth is that no school can guarantee it will stay Covid free. Even with multiple protective measures in place, bringing students back to schools will lead to new infections. If you can accept that this is bound to happen, then you can focus on what really matters:the safety measures your school will take when new cases emerge.

There is one other piece of advice I give to everyone who asks — listen to what the virus is telling you. If the virus is spreading widely and rapidly in your community, you cannot risk heading back to the classroom.

I often talk about it in terms of the weather. What do you do when a hurricane or tornado warning is in full effect? You head to the safest part of your home and you hunker down until the danger has passed. That's how we have to think about this pandemic. The Harvard Global Health Institute created a color-coded Covid risk map. The colors show you how high the risk of infection is in your community — red means the risk is extremely high, orange is high risk, yellow is moderate, and green is for areas that have near zero infections. At the end of July 2020, the map looked like this:

William A. Haseltine, PhD

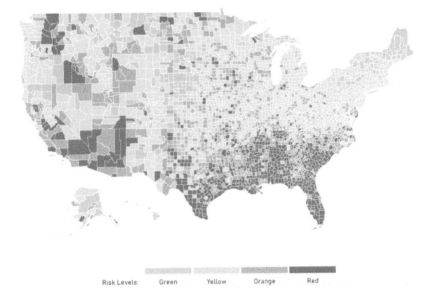

Figure 1. Harvard Global Health Institute Covid risk map
Source: Harvard Global Health Institute

If your community is in red, it means the hurricane is coming — gather your loved ones around you, stay home, and stay safe. If your community is orange, think of it like a thunderstorm. It's dangerous outside. You may not need to head to the bunker but you shouldn't risk going outside unless absolutely necessary. Areas in yellow have a heavy rain pouring down. You wouldn't head outside in the midst of a rainstorm without a raincoat, boots and your umbrella. Same goes for the pandemic — unless you're fully geared up with a mask, gloves, and hand sanitizer I wouldn't recommend you step outdoors. If you're in the green, consider it a sunny day — go out, enjoy, but remember to keep a watchful eye for clouds on the horizon.

When you think about these risks in relation to schools, my advice is simple — don't send your students to school in the midst of a hurricane or thunderstorm. If your state or county is in the red or orange, there should be no doubt about your choice — whether schools in your community are open or not, children should not return to class. I know keeping students at home is not an easy choice and for some may not even be possible, but I feel it is my responsibility to highlight the real risk to you and your family of returning to school when your region is in the red.

For areas in yellow and green, the risk of infection may be slightly less, but it is still there. The risk Covid poses to children and families is no small thing. Every day I see stories about Covid outbreaks in daycare centers and child care facilities across the country. I know from my study of the virus that each story of a new infection is also a story of a life permanently changed by this disease. Even those who show no sign of illness are at times left with damage to the lungs that may lead to longer term health issues.[i]

I also know keeping children out of school can be equally detrimental to the health and wellbeing of families. Schools play a fundamental role in a child's development. It's more than a venue for academic achievement. Our schools are the places where our children learn how to interact with the world around them and, for some, the sole source for healthy meals and the only safe and supportive environment they have.

I too wish for schools to reopen. But they should only reopen if they can do it safely and in a way that protects the health of all students, staff, and loved ones at home. Throughout all my research, I have only found one comprehensive report that includes all the guidance needed to reopen schools safely. That report, from the National Academies of Sciences, Engineering and Medicine, is written for school administrators and local district leaders as they think through their reopening plans.

But there is still nothing to help parents and students make the right decision for themselves and their families. I created the *Covid Back to School Guide* to fill this void. The information included here comes not just from the National

Academies report, but numerous case studies, policy briefs, peer-reviewed scientific journals, and best practices in education.

Right now this guide is focused primarily on public schools servings students from kindergarten to grade 12. The situation for students attending private schools and colleges is very different. While I leave these issues unaddressed today, rest assured that, as a "living book," I will be continually updating the text to address these and other issues tomorrow. Indeed the entire guide will be updated regularly to reflect current events and the latest research, and to keep pace with our ever-changing reality.

CHAPTER 1:

A Critical Need to Reopen Schools

Everyone — myself, my children, and my grandchildren included — wants students back in school. Kids crave it, parents need it, and local and national leaders view it as a critical step on the path to full reopening.

We know how important school is to the millions of students who attend. Classrooms are where our students learn how to gather and process new information.[ii] Lunch halls and schoolyards are where children learn how to manage emotions, stand up for themselves, and practice self control. Schools are so much more than a place of learning. They are second only to the home in their power to shape young hearts and minds —

laying the groundwork for social and emotional skills that will lead to better health, and a better future, down the line.[iii]

Closing down schools has long been part of our efforts to stop the spread of disease. Growing up in the oppressive heat of the Mojave Desert, I remember being turned away from the public pools and movie theaters that promised cool relief. The virus, polio, was very different, but the fear we felt was the same. So it was during the 1918 flu pandemic as well. That fall, nearly every public school in the United States closed its doors. Some remained shuttered for as long as five months.[iv]

For children who lack safety, comfort, and nourishment in their own homes, schools are sanctuaries, which is why many viewed the decision to shut them down last spring as a necessary evil. Once the outbreak was under control, schools would be among the first places to reopen—or so we hoped. Now that August is upon us and Covid case counts are reaching new heights, going back to school is no longer a given. That school closures slow the spread of disease is a proven fact, and Covid is likely no exception.[v]

But when parents can no longer send their children to school, problems otherwise unrelated to the disease arise, affecting everything from household income and employment to emotional and mental wellbeing. The majority of parents, many of whom had to quit their jobs or cut back on hours due to Covid-related school shutdowns, are burnt out from juggling competing demands of work, life, and remote learning.[vi] Parents aren't the only ones who suffer these consequences; children, too, are struggling to cope.[vii]

For all these reasons and more, one thing is clear: schools need to reopen. However, they also need to be safe. Guidelines released in March by the U.S. Centers for Disease Control and Prevention (CDC), the national health authority in the United States, were meant to help schools achieve this goal. But as of July 23, a revised version of the guidelines—made more lenient in response to political pressure from the White House—has replaced the original, sending mixed messages to school administrators, parents, students, and everyone in between.

The revised CDC guidelines stand firmly in favor of reopening schools this fall, but they lack the depth and clarity that might actually assist teachers and staff in keeping their classrooms safe. Social distancing is still recommended, for example, but any mention of "six feet apart" is gone. Also absent are instructions on what to do in the event of a "substantial, uncontrolled" outbreak—many parents' greatest fear. Were this to come true, experts agree that immediate shutdowns would be necessary. The CDC, on the other hand, deems school closures an "important consideration" only.

Recommendations this vague not only ring hollow, but put us in real danger. They read as suggestions, not hard and fast rules—leaving the door wide open for the kinds of missteps and oversights that will leave us vulnerable to infection. If our governments and school boards can't protect us from the health crisis at hand, it falls on parents like us to equip ourselves with the knowledge we need to keep our children and our communities safe.

Until the pandemic is over for good, the question of whether your child can return to school safely will never be simple. What this book can do is simplify the steps you need to take to arrive at an answer. Where to begin, you ask? With the subject of the next chapter: knowing your community.

CHAPTER 2:

Know Your Community

What is the community risk?

To both understand and avoid the risks of sending your child back to school, the first thing you must learn is how Covid is affecting your community on a daily basis. Until this disease is no longer a threat, consider yourself to be living in a hurricane zone—the threat of a hurricane is always there, but always changing and difficult to predict.

Just as a morning weather report, with its daily highs and lows and chance of rain, tells us whether we should wear a coat or bring an umbrella when we leave the house, certain

16

measures of Covid's spread and containment can tell us whether we should take more or less precautions on any given day. And just as the forecast of an imminent hurricane is reason enough to drop everything and stay home, so too are sharp or steady increases in the numbers I describe below.

If there are zero Covid infections in your community, you will no doubt feel more comfortable going back to school. Unfortunately for many of us, this is not the case—not in most parts of the world, and not in any part of the United States. In many states, single-day death counts and numbers of new infections are breaking records and reaching all-time highs. No matter where we live, we must ask ourselves: if I leave my house and spend some time out in my community, what is the risk that I'll get infected? If

I can't avoid exposure, what can I do to avoid infection?

If you live in a community where the number of new infections recorded each day is climbing rapidly, or where not enough testing is happening for that number to be accurate, you must be extremely careful. Without widespread testing, public health officials can't grasp the full extent of an outbreak. Remember: the faster and further a virus is spreading in your community, the higher the chance that the disease will break out in your school.

There are a few ways to determine the risk of Covid in your community. One is to look at the daily number of new confirmed cases per 100,000 people. Try to find this information at the smallest scale possible. That might be your county, or it might be your zip code. A lot can change from one zip code to the next. In order to make the best decision, you need the information most relevant to you. Many cities and states provide this information directly on their websites. If they don't, you can calculate it yourself with ease.

Some cities, like San Francisco, provide the number of new cases per 10,000 people by zip code.

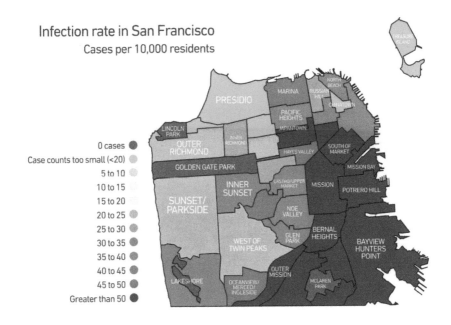

Figure 2. Infection rate in San Francisco
Source: DataSF

In this case, all you need to do is multiply that number by 10. If your city doesn't provide that amount of detail, here is what you can do:

How to calculate daily new cases per 100,000 people in your zip code

1. Go to https://www.unitedstateszipcodes.org/ and look up your zip code. Click the Population button and write down the population size.
2. Look up the daily number of confirmed Covid cases in your zip code and write it down, too.
3. Take the daily number of confirmed Covid cases, divide it by the total population size and multiply it by 100,000.

A high number of confirmed cases per 100,000 means the virus is spreading rapidly. Something to keep in mind is that these numbers only count the cases that have been *officially* confirmed—in other words, people who completed a genomic PCR test for Covid and got a positive result. For every confirmed case of Covid, there are likely many more that go undetected. Research conducted in Spain[viii] and across the United States[ix] using antibody tests reveal that the number of people who were or had been infected far exceeded officially recorded numbers. In some locations, the new numbers were ten times as high.

What this means for the risk of Covid in your community is that the number of infections you see on paper is only the tip of the iceberg. To get a better idea of the true number of infections in your community—including people who are asymptomatic or just beginning to develop symptoms—take that number and multiply it by 10. As of this writing, there are 4.29 million confirmed Covid cases in the United States. Think about it: the real total could be as high as 42.9 million!

Risk level	Daily new cases per 100,000 people
Low	Less than 1
Moderate	1-9
High	10-24
Very high	25+

Figure 3. Harvard Global Health Institute Covid risk ratings

Source: Harvard Global Health Institute

In addition to keeping track of the number of infections, you must learn more about the **testing capacity** in your community. If testing capacity is too limited, which means it would be either difficult or impossible for you to get tested if you needed to, public health authorities won't have the data they need to accurately track the spread of infections. If testing capacity is high and tests are widely available, it becomes much easier to detect new spikes and outbreaks.

To determine testing capacity, it's not enough to know the number of tests being conducted each day. In Haskell, Oklahoma, where the population is just under 2,000, conducting 250 tests a day might give public health authorities all the data they need to know where and how the disease is spreading. But in a major metropolis like Chicago, the same number would indicate a massive shortage.

Instead, look for the **positive test rate** in your community—the number of tests that, of all those being conducted, come back positive. A high positive test rate is any number over 5%. If the positive test rate is high, it tends to mean that the virus is spreading rapidly within your community, or that only the patients who feel sick enough to seek care at a clinic or hospital are getting tested. In either case, it means testing isn't widespread enough to identify new cases or to truly measure the scope of the outbreak.

If your community has a low positive test rate—anything 5% or below, but the closer to zero the better—then you can be more confident that enough testing is going on for public health authorities to make good decisions about safety and reopening.

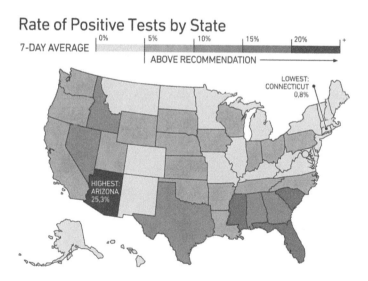

Figure 4. Rate of positive tests in the United States by state

Source: The Covid Tracking Project

If you learn and continue checking both the infection rate and the positive test rate in your community, you'll have a better understanding of how the disease is spreading and your risk of being exposed. Another piece of the puzzle that isn't as critical but may be useful is **hospital capacity**, which involves measures like the amount of space available in intensive care units (ICUs) for patients in need of critical care.

If infection rates and positive test rates are low, it will be unlikely that local ICUs are full. But with a disease like Covid, which can keep severely ill patients in the hospital for up to two months, it is a possibility.[x] Should you or your family fall ill, you'll want to know whether nearby hospitals have enough beds and equipment to provide adequate care.

Once you're up to date on cases per 100,000 people, testing capacity, and hospital capacity, there remains one final measure that can improve your understanding of risk in your community: **disease monitoring**, or how your community is tracking and tracing new infections.

Monitoring an infectious disease outbreak is crucial to containing it, and one tried and true method of doing this is **contact tracing**. In countries where Covid is now contained, disease monitoring efforts have deployed a combination of contact tracing and voluntary or mandatory isolation.

This is how contact tracing works. First, when someone tests positive for Covid infection, they're asked to identify the people they've been in contact with over the past few days. Next, a team of public health officials and volunteers called contact tracers is dispatched to locate those recent contacts and inform them of their recent exposure. Last but not least, the contacts are asked to isolate themselves for at least two weeks so any potential infection they may have isn't passed on to anyone else. If they end up developing symptoms, they notify the contact tracing team—and the process begins again.

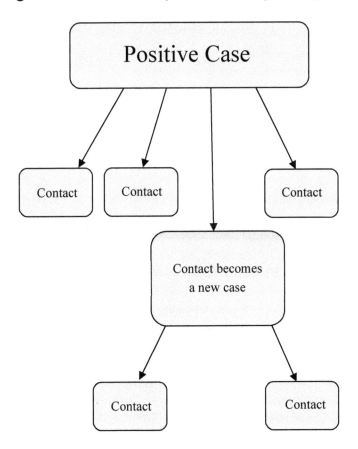

Figure 5. How contact tracing works

Once a verified list of contacts is obtained from an infected person, ideally contact tracers would be in touch with every single person on the list within 24 hours. But in reality, this goal is rarely ever achieved. Sometimes the oversight is a matter of poor planning and management, in which case the public health officials themselves are at fault. But other times it has to do with things outside any health department's control. Patients might not remember everyone they were in contact with or feel uncomfortable providing full names and numbers, while their contacts might simply miss the contact tracer's call.

Looking into a few metrics related to contact tracing can give you a sense of the quality of your community's disease monitoring efforts. These include the number of patients who tested positive for Covid and were interviewed by contact tracers within 24 hours; the percentage of those contacts that were reached and informed of their recent exposure within the same 24-hour period; and the number of contacts who actually quarantined for two weeks.

The problem is that very few states share this data publicly, which will make it a struggle for you to learn if a contact tracing program is working as it should. What you can do is see if any local newspapers or media outlets have already done the digging for you—in which case you can survey the numbers and judge for yourself whether enough disease monitoring is happening in your community to get ahead of the outbreak.

Key Takeaways

- You should check the risk of Covid in your community as often as you check the weather—on a daily basis. A significant rise in the number of new cases or a high positive test rate, like a severe weather warning, will demand more serious precautions.

- If the number of confirmed Covid cases per 100,000 people is below 1, you may be able to breath a sigh of relief. Any higher is a reason for concern.

- For a better sense of the true number of infections in your area — not just confirmed numbers — multiply the number on record by 10.

- The **positive test rate** is the best measure of a community's **testing capacity**, not the number of tests conducted per day. A high positive test rate is any number above 5%.

- A good measure of **hospital capacity** is the number of beds available in intensive care units (ICUs).

- One way to inspect the quality of **disease monitoring** in your community is to learn about your local **contact tracing** program.

Questions to Consider

The number of infections in my community is considered high, should a student attend school? When the number of infections is high, school buildings should remain closed and students should only learn remotely. If some school districts choose to stay open for in-person learning, it may be tempting and sometimes necessary for a student to return to the classroom, but it is by no means recommended. The student faces a real risk of infection and so does the student's family at home. Despite the very real challenges and distress that remote learning may cause, it is safer for the student to remain at home.

The number of infections in my community is considered moderate, should a student attend school? The answer to this one isn't straightforward. If your school is taking the precautions described in the next chapter of this book, and if the student and his or her immediate family are not at risk for severe Covid, it may be safe for a student to return to school for some in-person learning. If the student or any of the student's family members are at risk of becoming severely ill if infected, you may want to opt for remote learning instead.

The number of infections in my community is low, does this mean a student can return to school safely? It definitely means a return to school is safer than if the infection rate in your community was high, but a lot will depend on whether most students at the school come from the same community. If your school attracts students from across your city or from a wide variety of communities, it's important for you to know the infection rate from all the areas where students and staff will be coming from. If they are all relatively low, the risk of infection for students will be limited.

There aren't many new cases of Covid in my community but the positive test rate is high, is it safe for a student to attend school in person? I would not recommend going back to the classroom when the positive test rate in your community is high, no matter what the infection rate, hospital capacity, or other measures may be. A high positive test rate suggests either that the outbreak is widespread, or that not enough testing is being done to know if it is. Until the positive test rate comes down, it is safer for students to stay at home.

There's no information about our contact tracing program available. If all other indicators suggest it's safe, is it okay for a student to return to school? If your city lacks a robust contact tracing program, it is riskier to return to school. There are measures your school may be able to put into place to mitigate the risk. These measures are discussed in Chapter 4: Know Your School.

CHAPTER 3:

Know Your Risk

Would sending my child back to school put me and my family at risk?

You've probably seen the headlines claiming that kids are not only less likely to catch the virus than adults, but less likely to spread it as well. These are the claims that some politicians and members of the press have been using to justify reopening schools even when the disease is surging across the country. The need to get students back into the classroom, they say, far outweighs the risks Covid presents to them and their families.

Of course we want to believe that no harm will come to our children if they're allowed to return to school—that even if they catch the virus, they won't spread it to us. What the headlines fail to mention, however, is that many of the studies they cite were conducted mid-lockdown.[xi] With schools shuttered and playgrounds closed, most children were almost entirely sheltered in the safety of their homes. Naturally they were less likely to become infected than their parents, who had no choice but to venture out for groceries or essential work.[xii]

That children were homebound for months isn't the only caveat to keep in mind when we hear they aren't vulnerable to Covid. New research out of Italy shows that infected children have at least as much of the virus in their noses and throats as infected adults. In fact, children under the age of five may have up to 100 times more of the virus in those areas than adults.[xiii] The research also indicates that kids can easily spread the disease to others. In fact, they may be more infectious than any other group. After looking at nearly 1,500 confirmed cases of Covid, the researchers found that the highest rate of contagiousness of any age group was among those 5 to 10 years old. And that level of contagiousness occurred when schools were closed, not when classes were in session and children mingled freely. The lowest rate of contagiousness was among those between 30 and 49.

Characteristic of Case	Cases	Number of Contacts	Number of Contacts who Became Cases	Contagiousness
Age, Years (n=1,489)				
0-14	14	49	11	22.4%
25-29	118	475	62	13.1%
30-49	446	2,361	250	10.6%
50-64	477	2,222	303	13.6%
65-74	181	559	85	15.2%
75+	253	909	155	17.1%

Gender (n=1,442)	727	3,427	414	12.1%
Women	715	2,973	416	14.0%
Men				

Table 1. Contagiousness of index cases by age and gender, Province of Trento -- March-April 2020

Source: Contact Tracing during Phase I of the COVID-19 Pandemic in the Province of Trento, Italy: Key Findings and Recommendations

All it takes to start a chain of transmission is one student, one infection, that sparks an outbreak that spirals out of control. As alarming as this possibility may be, some of us may take small comfort in the fact that a school outbreak would, at the very least, spare our children from the worst symptoms Covid has to offer—namely, the damage to the lungs, heart, and other vital organs that puts people in hospitals. Sadly, this isn't guaranteed. While the majority of children who get sick or infected with Covid develop either mild symptoms or none at all, there have been instances in which a Covid infection triggered something much worse: **multisystem inflammatory syndrome in children (MIS-C)**.

Multisystem inflammatory syndrome in children (MIS-C) is a new disease that can appear in children infected with Covid. This can happen to anyone from age 0 to 20, and occasionally beyond, but it is most common among kids age 7 or 8. A child with MIS-C tends to start showing symptoms several weeks after they have been exposed to the Covid virus, and generally two to four weeks after someone close to the child tests positive.

Children with MIS-C usually don't have any respiratory symptoms.[xiv] Instead, they experience symptoms that can be confusing to assess— impaired brain function, headaches, muscle weakness, and reduced reflexes. A child may appear to be entirely normal one moment, then faint the next. In some cases, MIS-C leads to loss of speech, loss of coordination, and mental confusion.

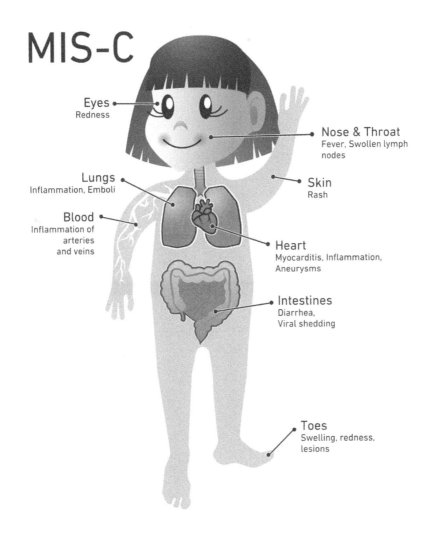

Figure 6. What MIS-C does to children

Children who live with other medical conditions, such as neurologic, genetic, and metabolic conditions or congenital heart disease, have the greatest risk of becoming extremely sick from Covid and experiencing MIS-C. Thankfully, MIS-C can be treated, but at the first sign of the disease you must take your child to the hospital immediately.

While the Covid pandemic dates back to January, the first cases of MIS-C didn't appear until many months later in May. We're so used to speaking and hearing about Covid that sometimes we forget how relatively new the disease is—and how many of its mysteries we've yet to solve. So far we know that Covid can take an enormous toll on the body, affecting every major organ and leading to lifelong impairments. Even cases that seem mild on the surface can leave behind long-term injuries in their wake.

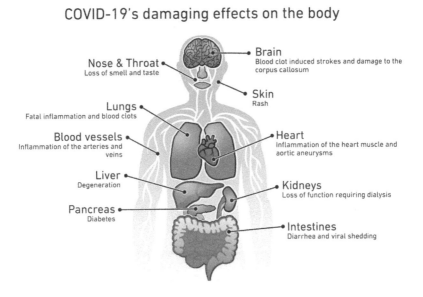

Figure 7. What Covid does to adults

Phases of COVID-19

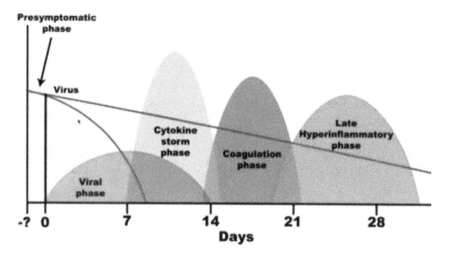

Figure 8. Four phases of Covid-19

Source: COVID-19 Testing: How Long Is Someone Infectious Enough To Be Able to Spread The Virus? How to Limit Undetected Infectious Days?

When deciding whether or not your child should go back to school, remember to consider the risks Covid poses to yourself and the rest of your household. Nearly 3.5 million older adults over the age of 65—one of the groups at greatest risk of becoming severely ill from Covid—live with a school age child.[xv] People with underlying conditions like asthma, diabetes, and heart disease are also at higher risk. Reopening schools and returning to classrooms won't just affect the students. It will affect every parent, grandparent, sibling, and friend who lives with them, too. Here we lay out the major risk factors for adults and children.

Risk Factors for Adults

Age	• Risk of severe illness increases with age • 60 and older are considered high risk • 85 and older are at the greatest risk
Pre-existing Medical Conditions	• Cancer • Chronic kidney disease • COPD (chronic obstructive pulmonary disease)

	• Immunocompromised • Obesity • Critical heart conditions • Sickle cell disease • Type 2 diabetes mellitus
Other factors that may increase risk	• Other medical conditions like asthma, hypertension, dementia or other neurologic conditions, weakened immune system, liver disease, pregnancy, type 1 diabetes, pulmonary fibrosis, and people with developmental or behavioral disorders • Smoking • Homelessness

Table 2. Covid risk factors for adults
Source: U.S. Centers for Disease Control

Risk Factors for Children

Age	<ul><li>Infants younger than 1 year are at higher risk than older children</li></ul>
Pre-existing Medical Conditions	<ul><li>Chronic lung disease (including asthma)</li><li>Cardiovascular disease</li><li>Immunosuppression</li></ul>

Table 3. Covid risk factors for children
Source: U.S. Centers for Disease Control

Key Takeaways

- Before deciding whether or not to send your child back to school, you need to know your **personal risk**: how dangerous the virus is for you and your household.

- Claims that children aren't as likely to catch or spread the virus may have some truth to them, but they don't tell the full story.

- Kids age 10 and under aren't as infectious as adults, but kids over the age of 10 are.

- While children rarely become very sick from Covid, those who do sometimes develop a condition called **multisystem inflammatory syndrome in children (MIS-C)**. MIS-C is extremely dangerous. If your child has MIS-C symptoms, take them to the hospital immediately.

- In many ways, Covid is still a mysterious new disease. We're learning about how it damages the bodies of people of all ages. Until we know more, no one is safe.

- If a Covid outbreak occurs at school, there is a chance the disease will be brought into your home. This is especially dangerous if you or anyone in your household is above the age of 65 or has an underlying health condition.

Questions to Consider

Here are some questions you can use to assess your personal risk before deciding whether your child should head back to school. You can also use them if you're an older high school or college student yourself and need to decide whether returning to the classroom is safe.

What grade is the student in? If the student is in elementary school, it may be safer to send them back to the classroom than if they are in junior high or high school. The risk of younger students becoming infected or spreading the infection is somewhat lower for younger students than junior and high school students. If the elementary school student shares a building with junior and senior high school students, you may want to rethink the risk, as it is more likely that outbreaks will occur among older students.

Is the child at high risk of severe complications due to a Covid-19 infection? If this is your family's situation, think very carefully before agreeing to send the child back to school. If you have no alternatives other than to return to the classroom, make sure the school staff is aware of the child's vulnerabilities to disease and make sure they will enforce social distancing strategies and provide the necessary protective equipment.

Are there members of your family who are at high risk of severe complications due to a Covid-19 infection? If your answer is yes, consider the age of the child or children who may be attending school. If the child is under the age of ten, it is possible that they won't raise your family's risk of infection significantly, even if someone tests positive in their school. If the child is over the age of ten, think carefully about whether you and your family can afford an increased risk of infection.

If someone in the child's class tests positive for Covid-19, do you have a safe space in your home to quarantine them from the rest of your family? Because Covid is highly infectious, anyone who has been exposed to someone with the disease should consider themselves infected and begin isolating themselves immediately. If someone in the child's class tests positive, your child would ideally stay isolated in a bedroom in your home for two weeks to avoid infecting the rest of the family. No one should enter the room for any reason, and any food or garbage should be left at the door for a contactless exchange.

Some children are too young to quarantine alone. Others may be unable to quarantine effectively because of the layout of the home—sharing a bathroom would break the quarantine. If you think the child could quarantine effectively in your home, you may feel more comfortable with the risks associated with them being back at school.

CHAPTER 4:

Know Your School

———— ❧ ————

Is my school taking the right steps to keep our students safe?

No matter how safe we may feel in our communities or in our homes, we take a leap of faith when we send students back into classrooms. As much as we may trust our teachers to lead and mold young minds, can we really trust that they've been given the resources and training to keep students safe?

There are a multitude of questions school administrators will need to consider before reopening: How will they prevent infections? How will they identify new outbreaks? And — in what is a very probable scenario — what if a student shows some symptoms of Covid-19, but not all?

Unfortunately, these aren't simple questions with straightforward answers. Imagine this, a student in class has a fever and a cough. It could be Covid, or just a common cold. Ideally, that student would immediately be pulled out of class, brought to a safe and isolated space, and tested for Covid. If they test positive, all their classmates and teachers would be notified of their exposure and sent home to quarantine. If negative, everyone is allowed to stay.

Now think of how this would play out in practice in a country like the United States, where tests aren't a given and results can take up to two weeks to come back from a lab. Should all the student's classmates and teachers be sent home to quarantine as the school waits for the results to come in? What would working parents and siblings in school do during this time — stay home as well? If parents can't work from home, can they send their student to a family member's house or child care center safely? The questions are endless and answers few and far between.

In the absence of firm guidelines from the CDC, state departments of education, school districts, and individual schools themselves have essentially been left to their own devices to create their own plans. Whether those plans will offer enough protection for you and your student is ultimately something that only you can decide. But there are places you can look to guide you in finding those answers.

More than a dozen countries have successfully reopened their schools to children of all ages.[xvi] There are some basic measures that seem to have worked across the board: keeping student groups small and socially distanced, making sure students and staff all wear masks, and having strict protocols in place for when a student, teacher, or staff member tests positive or shows symptoms of Covid-19.[xvii]

Finland and Denmark both staggered their reopenings, bringing the youngest students back to school first, and holding some classes outdoors. Some school buildings were also upgraded, with improved ventilation and additional toilets and sinks installed.[xviii] In many parts of Asia, students have their temperature checked before they're allowed into class and are asked to keep their masks on at all times. During the times when students have to take them off, like at lunch, they are separated from each other by glass or plastic dividers[xix] or they're asked to sit and eat in silence to reduce the chance of spreading the virus.[xx] None of these efforts are ideal, but they are necessary to keep outbreaks at bay.

Even with all these measures in place, there have still been spikes in new cases at schools. Perhaps the most telling story comes from Israel where schools were quickly shut down just weeks after reopening. Studies found that hundreds of students and staff were initially infected in school, then the outbreaks spread to the general population.[xxi] Covid cases are now on an exponential rise across the country — a sobering lesson for all of us.

One important detail to keep in mind about all the countries who have reopened their schools successfully: their outbreaks were well under control before the doors to their classrooms opened. If the United States, Brazil or any other country still in the midst of a surge of infections sends students back to school, the results are likely to be far less promising. Think back to the Harvard Global Health Institute map earlier in this book. Countries that reopened schools were fully in the green when they reopened, not the patchwork of red and orange that the United States is in today.

If the U.S. successfully reopens its schools while tens of thousands of new Covid cases continue to be recorded each day, we will be the first country to do so. An impressive feat but one that won't come without a cost. Our schools today are not up to snuff when it comes to pandemic protections. Schools will need additional resources to stock their shelves with protective equipment, upgrade their ventilation and air filtration systems, and reorganize classrooms and school spaces to maximize capacity while reducing student and staff density.[xxii] This is far more than just buying everyone a few boxes of gloves and masks.

I've spoken to many parents and students this summer who have been desperate to know what their school is planning to do to keep students safe. The National Academies put together a list that explains what schools can be doing. The full list is included in the Appendix, but below is a shortened summary for you to consider.

Wearing Masks, Handwashing, and Cleaning

Covid is spread through respiratory droplets when people breathe, talk, cough, or sneeze around each other. Asking all students to wear masks is one of the most effective ways schools can reduce the spread of the virus. Respiratory droplets that land on surfaces can infect someone who touches the surface and then touches their mouth, nose, or eyes. Having students and staff wash their hands regularly with soap and water can help remove the virus. Regular cleaning is important to eliminate the virus on surfaces, especially for high touch areas and shared material.

Physical Distancing and Avoiding Large Gatherings

When people are in close contact, they can easily breathe in droplets containing the virus that other people have exhaled. Most droplets fall to the ground within three to six feet of being exhaled, so schools should maintain a distance of at least three feet and ideally six between students at all times. Large gatherings often bring students in close contact. If a person is sick, a large gathering can ignite a new outbreak that may quickly spread out of control. All assemblies and large sports events should be eliminated and large gatherings of students in common areas, like cafeterias, hallways, and entryways, avoided.

Ventilation and Air Filtration

While most droplets containing the virus fall out of the air, some can stay suspended in it for hours. If enough of these droplets accumulate in the air, they can pose a risk to anyone in the room. When fresh air is added to a room, the amount of virus in the room diminishes. Small rooms with poor ventilation are likely to increase risk of transmission but opening windows and doors or moving classes outdoors can reduce the risk to students. Improving air filtration systems by upgrading filters and preventing indoor air from recirculating is also important.

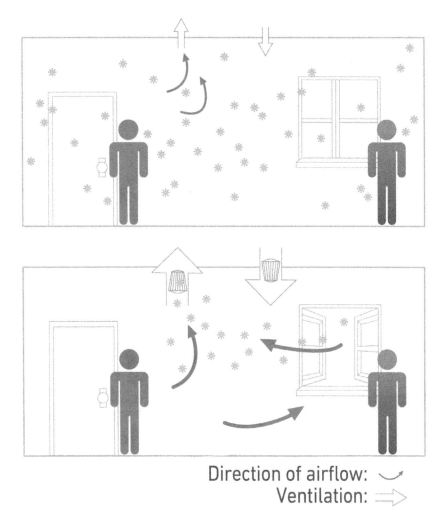

Direction of airflow: ⤵
Ventilation: ⟹

Figure 9. The benefits of ventilation and air filtration

Temperature Screening

The jury is still out on whether schools should prioritize temperature checks and symptom screening for students. More and more researchers are finding that people are contagious before they show symptoms, so checking for temperature alone won't stop the spread of the virus in school. Even if schools choose not to conduct temperature checks before students get on buses or enter the school, parents should be doing their own checks at home each day, no matter what.

School-based Contact Tracing and Quarantine

Even if a school lies within a community with its own contact tracing program, schools themselves should be ready to conduct their own contact tracing effort when a student in the school shows symptoms of Covid or tests positive. The contact tracing program would ideally look like the following figure.

Figure 10. How contact tracing works in schools

When a student or staff member tests positive or shows symptoms of Covid, school staff should immediately move the person to an isolated space and ask them about the people they have been in touch with recently, both in the school and outside of it — like at drop off, pick up or even at home on various playdates and group gatherings. Staff should also check school records to identify other students and staff members who were exposed, such as classmates, teachers, librarians, custodial staff, and other friends and parents outside the school.

The school should ensure that all those exposed are contacted and asked to stay home during a voluntary 14 day isolation period. None of those exposed should be allowed back onto school grounds during that two week period. The school should also be shut down temporarily so the building can be disinfected and sanitized. If a cluster of new infections emerges, the entire school should be closed for a minimum of two weeks and, ideally, until the outbreak in the community is known to be back under control.

Key Takeaways

- Schools that reopened successfully did it when the outbreaks in their country and community were under control. If the outbreak in your community is not under control, **do not head back into the classroom**.

- Wearing masks can significantly reduce the spread of disease. At a minimum, make sure your school will be **enforcing mask-wearing** among all students and staff. You should also make sure there is a plan in place to keep students apart at the lunch hour, when the masks come off.

- It's important for you to understand what **other strategies** your school will implement to keep students safe, especially in terms of social distancing, routine handwashing, and plans for large gatherings.

- Only rigorous **contact tracing and quarantine** can prevent new infections at your school from turning into full blown outbreaks. Be sure you understand exactly what your school will do if someone shows symptoms of Covid or tests positive.

Questions to Consider

How can I be sure my school will protect students from infection? Your school should be open and transparent about the strategies they are putting in place to protect students. At a minimum, schools should be enforcing mask wearing, routine hand hygiene, and physical distancing. Common areas and large school gatherings in cafeterias, gyms, or recess halls should be cancelled until the outbreak is under control across the nation. Your school should also ensure that no one with a fever or any other symptom of Covid is allowed onto school grounds. If your school is not meeting this bare minimum standard, you should consider other alternatives than a return to school, if possible.

What protocols should my school put in place to handle a potential Covid case in the

school? When a student or staff member tests positive, the school should enforce their own contact tracing and quarantine program, as described earlier in this chapter. They should be able to answer specific questions about their protocol, such as whether siblings of students who were exposed will need to be quarantined and whether the quarantine will apply only when a student tests positive or even when a student shows symptoms. Ideally, schools should be erring on the side of caution despite the inconvenience this may cause for parents, students, and teachers alike. It's important that you take responsibility for notifying everyone in your circle of contacts, if you or your child is exposed. *Everyone* exposed should ideally quarantine themselves.

What about transportation to school? Crowded or poorly ventilated school buses can be as much of a risk for students as crowded or poorly ventilated classrooms. If there's a possibility of traveling to school by foot, bicycle, scooter, or in a private vehicle, that would be the safer option. If the only option for the student is to take a school bus or public transportation, make sure they are wearing a mask and not touching common surfaces, and ensure there is adequate distance between passengers.

What questions should I be asking school administrators? The most important thing is to make sure you have a clear understanding of all the strategies your schools will be using to keep students safe. Ask them about the topics mentioned earlier in the chapter — mask wearing, handwashing routines, school cleanings, social distancing, ventilation, air filtration, temperature checks, and contact tracing — but probe what other strategies they'll be incorporating. Will they stagger school schedules for students in different grades? Conduct some classes outdoors? Create a special quarantine space? Provide counseling for students who aren't coping well with the new rules? The more information you have, the more comfortable you'll be with your final decision.

CHAPTER 5:

Remote Learning and Other Opportunities To Learn

———✦———

O ne of my greatest fears is that schools will reopen in communities where Covid is still circulating widely. If this is the case for you, I cannot stress how important it is for you to seriously consider the risk at hand. If I were giving advice to my own children or grandchildren in this situation, I would tell them to stay home.

I know that staying home is not a viable proposition for every student or their families. It is a sacrifice — one which risks affecting the financial, mental, and emotional wellbeing of the entire family unit. Staying home and learning remotely is a luxury only afforded to a lucky few.

Many parents work for companies that reject outright the notion of working remotely, making staying home to care for younger students near impossible. Others have chosen vocations deemed essential and are required even in the midst of the worst pandemic to commute into work. If you are in this situation, I encourage you to download a copy of my *Family Guide to Covid,* available for free on my website (www.covidfamilyguide.com). There I offer tips to protect yourselves and those you love.

For those who have the flexibility to learn at home, this chapter offers advice on how to overcome some of the mental and physical challenges that come with at-home learning.

Learning environments

To learn, students need focus. And to focus, students need space. Whether it's a private room or a quiet corner of the house, designate certain spots for learning and instruct all members of the household to respect those boundaries. Tuck away potential distractions, like phones, and try to keep noise levels to a minimum whenever you're near.

Students also need breaks, especially when lessons involve lots of screentime. In between classes or study sessions, encourage your child to stand up, step away from the computer, and stretch. If they're younger and feeling restless, a dance break or even roughhousing with a family member will allow them to expend some of that pent-up energy. Without interruptions here and there, one subject will bleed into another, making it difficult for students to retain information.

Learning after hours

Outside of virtual class time, a simple strategy to stay on top of tasks is to create a daily schedule. Being at home and away from the rigorous academic environment at school can certainly make students feel less motivated to complete their assignments. Making a schedule that incorporates tasks, breaks, and other goals for the day is a great way for students to stay organized and manage their time as they work through the checklist.

Virtual study sessions and group Zoom calls with friends to talk about homework is also a great way for students to stay connected and engaged. Together, students can brainstorm other ideas to stay motivated, like working together on flashcards, study schedules, and mock tests.

Virtual resources

Students may miss the richness of learning in an in-person environment, but there are a wide variety of virtual resources that can help fill part of the void left when one learns alone at home. Khan Academy and HippoCampus offer a wide variety of educational resources on a multitude of subject areas. For younger learners, resources like Dreambox, Prodigy and BrainPOP provide interactive, self-paced online learning environments that help students learn new concepts and practice previously learned skills. Online tutoring services may also be a useful bridge between the familiarity of the classroom and the potentially unwelcome novelty of learning at home and independently.

Pressure

The pressure of lockdowns and school closures and the isolation that comes with both can be hard to manage. It's okay if you're feeling sad, scared, frustrated, or angry. We know that the lack of social interaction and outdoor activities caused by the pandemic is linked to increased depression among students.[xxiii] We also know that most students feel they need mental health support to deal with the challenges that come with remote learning and school shutdowns.[xxiv]

If and when schools reopen, the pressure on students continuing to learn remotely will only increase. Sitting home alone while your classmates are together with teachers is no easy feat. There are, thankfully, many online resources that can help relieve the pressure, including some like Nod created specifically for students. Other resources like All Mental Health, Calm, and

Headspace provide resources that are applicable to parents and students alike, such as meditations, relaxation exercises, and explanations of coping strategies specific to Covid.

These are uncertain times for all of us. The mere recognition that no one is alone in their struggles may be the best first step to bringing some small relief in these challenging times.[xxv]

Key Takeaways

- Create a **positive learning environment** free of distractions and set up a routine that gives adequate time for learning and for mental breaks.

- Even though remote learning may not be your ideal situation, try to make good use of all the **education resources available online**. You may not be allowed back in the classroom but learning virtually can still open doors to new experiences and opportunities for connection.

- It's okay to feel frustrated or angry at the current situation. If you're having a hard time controlling your emotions, look for **online mental health support**. Or maybe just call a friend or talk to a family member. Simply acknowledging your feelings and sharing your challenges may be the best first step you didn't know you needed.

CHAPTER 6:

Personal Strategies

———— ❧ ————

In the last five chapters, you learned about three levels of risk, got a crash course on remote learning, asked yourself some big questions, and hopefully arrived at some helpful answers—all of which can help you prepare for the fall.

Now it's time to learn some personal strategies for keeping students safe and well in the months to come. Many of these are discussed in my companion book, *A Family Guide to Covid*, available for free on my website (www.covidfamilyguide.com).

Keeping clean: handwashing and social distancing

Under lockdown and over the summer, washing hands regularly and staying six feet away from strangers was easy enough. But when school is back in session, it's easy to imagine a situation where students, especially younger students, forget all the guidance drilled into them in recent months, putting themselves at risk.

As students prepare to go back to school, it's important to remember the basics — handwashing, hand sanitizing, and keeping hands away from the face. If you didn't explain why these behaviors matter before, now might be a good time.

Suiting up: wearing masks and face shields

Whether it's surgical masks you bought at your local pharmacy or cloth face covers you make at home, wearing a mask to school—and keeping it on for the whole school day—will make a huge difference in preventing the spread of disease. Another option to consider is face shields, especially for students who wear glasses or find face masks extremely uncomfortable.

More than back-to-school jitters: coping with Covid-related moods

Some students might be delighted by the idea of going back to school, but others are bound to feel more fear and anxiety than excitement. Most will likely feel a mix of all of the above, which can be difficult to navigate. Try to stay aware of these changing moods and open up avenues to talk about tough subjects, like depression, anger, and resentment.

Staying informed: checking Covid risk like the weather

Remember the measures of community risk— infection rate, testing capacity, and so on—we discussed in Chapter 2? Make a habit of checking these stats, ideally at the zip code level, as often as you check the weather. Find websites that provide this information, bookmark them, and visit them every day like clockwork.

If you notice a spike, take note and recognize that you might need a plan of action in case things go haywire. If school is in session, give your administrators a call and ask them some of the questions included in Chapter 4.

Spreading the word: educating yourself and the people around you

This global pandemic started with just one person, and this has been the case in every community it has spread to since. Until not a single person in your community has Covid, the risk of another outbreak will remain—whether you live in a small town of 2,000 people or a big city of 2 million.

In the meantime, continue to seek out information about Covid and share it with others, especially other parents and students in your community. Consider starting a group chat or Facebook group for community Covid updates if none already exist. Such hubs can not only be a convenient way to stay on top of local updates, but a place to have meaningful conversations about what your school is doing right or wrong to reopen.

Epilogue

M y greatest hope is that this *Back To School Guide* has given you new insight into the potential risks of returning to school. I should hope that no one reading this book walks away from it thinking that I am against the reopening of our schools. Far from it.

I, like every other parent and grandparent, hope that schools reopen and kids return to the nurturing arms of their teachers and the classroom environments that will help them flourish and thrive. But no school should open if they can't open safely. And today in America, I would hazard to say that no public school is ready to open its doors.

While parents and students carry the heavy burden of making the final decision about reentering the classroom, the responsibility for keeping students safe doesn't lie solely with you, nor does it lie entirely in the hands of school administrators and staff. In the end, it's our government who should ensure kids are safe at school.

The fact that there are no clear and consistent guidelines for reopening schools in the United States is a tremendous governmental failure. Our leaders have been bogged down in debates over politics instead of focusing on the public health priorities needed to contain the outbreak and to keep the youngest and most precious among us safe.

The results of these failings are seen in the stories we read about today in our schools. In the last week of July 2020, students in some central

Indiana schools returned for in-person classes. They were among the first in the nation to do so. The first day the school district reopened, they counted their first case of Covid-19 — a junior high school student spent a half day in class before results from a Covid test showed he was infected.[xxvi] After hours in class, the student was isolated and contacts were called, but is that really enough? In my opinion, not in the least.

Public schools in America need many more resources to handle positive Covid cases and keep them from spreading. Some suggest that the cost for school districts to implement the necessary strategies might be nearly $2 million per district. You can see the full breakdown in the Appendix, but it boils down to about $615 dollars per student. If governments don't step in with education bailouts that are on par with their economic bailouts, we will suffer tragedies far greater than we have suffered to date.

Children and younger adults are not immune from infection and no one should fool themselves into thinking they are. But just because children can fall ill, it doesn't mean we can't protect them. We know what we need to do to stop Covid-19 from spreading in our schools and across our communities at large. What we need now is the commitment to get the job done.

I encourage each of you reading this book to call on your local and national leaders and ask them to put their politics aside so we can focus on supporting our children and returning them safely to the schools and the communities they love so much. I leave you now not with my own words, but rather with reflections from students and parents around the world who share in the selfsame struggle as you — is it really the right thing to head back to school?

Shreya Kavuru, High School Student, New Hampshire, USA

After being cooped up in my house for more than four months, there is nothing I would rather do than sit in my dorm common room with my friends, doing homework with the periodic pauses of rolling on the ground from laughing so hard at the random stories we share with each other.

Going from practically living with my friends at boarding school to not seeing them for almost half a year was an abrupt and unexpected change. Personally, I would love to go back to school. I miss my friends, my dorm, and the dorm members more than anything.

I have lived in the same dorm for three years now, and I have never felt more at home than in that place. What I love about my dorm is its inviting nature. My two friends, who live in rooms right next to mine, make it clear that their doors are always open if I ever want to talk. All the girls in my dorm are the exact same way; they are extremely supportive of one another and will always be there for each other, whether as a person to confide in or a person who has a box full of snacks to distribute.

Not only do I miss my friends, but I miss the environment of the school itself. I like keeping myself busy and moving around. A typical school day for me usually consists of going to classes, having lunch, attending office hours, playing sports, eating dinner, having club meetings, and doing homework. I have grown so accustomed to this lifestyle that being away from it has made me feel like I am not myself. When school became virtual, I thought I would fall back into the groove

I so missed. But between constantly clicking on various Zoom links, staring at a screen, and sitting in the same spot for five to six hours, it just was not the same.

While there are many reasons why I long to go back, I also have quite a few concerns about returning to campus. I know my school is planning on creating its own bubble and is taking the necessary precautions to bring students back in a safe manner. However, the biggest worry I have is that there will be an asymptomatic student who will have a false negative test. In my school, you are bound to see everyone either in passing or at meals. When a virus is going around, many people are bound to catch it. Two years ago, flu season was so bad that cots had to be placed on the tennis courts to accommodate everyone who had the flu. My fear is that if one person is infected with Covid, they will spread it to everyone within a matter of days. The danger doesn't stop with the students. Since my school is 100% residential, all the faculty and staff live there as well. That means the virus could spread to the faculty and staff, who may have existing health conditions, or to their families, which may include older adults or young kids. Knowing this is a possibility makes me wary of going back to school.

Additionally, while my school will require everyone to wear masks and practice social distancing, it is hard to enforce such rules in the dorms. Normally, for public school or day students at private schools, they can take off their masks and stop social distancing once they are in the comforts of their own homes. However, for someone like me who lives on campus, it is hard to put these safety measures in place for the whole school at all times, each day and every day.

Something else that I worry about is not getting the full school experience if I go back to campus. With all these precautions in place, I may not be able to eat meals with my friends if my school staggers meal times for everyone and sets up various meal locations. Additionally, I won't be able to sleep over in my friends' dorms, play sports, or go to school dances or other Saturday night activities that all the students look forward to. I understand that these are the necessary steps we must take to make sure everyone is safe, but at the same time, it will be difficult to physically be at school but not actually feel like I am there, experiencing everything to the fullest as I normally would have.

This is a very difficult and uncertain time for everyone, and I know that schools are doing what they can to return to some version of normalcy. But as a student, I have very conflicting feelings about going back to school, and I know I'm not alone. While we do want to return to campus to see our friends, go to classes in person, play sports, and participate in extracurricular activities, it is not as simple as that. We must also be aware of what will be changing and factor in these changes when deciding if we want to go back to school or not.

I would love to get back to my normal life at school, but I know that we still have ways to go before everything returns to just that: normal.

"Should I stay or should I go?" The Clash, 1981

We are a family of five, living in the paradise bubble of Laguna Beach, California. The pandemic has more or less passed us by, or so we thought. On March 13 Governor Newsom announced his lock-down and our family settled into the new experiment. As a parent, I was thrilled. Finally, dinner together every day, puzzles, scrabble, home improvement projects, learning Mandarin, family cooking sessions, and a whole new opportunity to connect on a deeper level with our children. Home schooling was surely going to be easier and more effective than our local public school could provide. The children saw things differently.

My oldest daughter, who is sixteen, blamed the pandemic on us as we informed her that she was forbidden from visiting her boyfriend. She disappeared into her basement level room and would only reappear to eat, scowl, and defy any attempt at direction or discipline from us. Our middle child just laughed when we presented him with his daily schedule and 3-month goal list. He would smile and agree to follow the rules, but then promptly go onto his Xbox, which quickly became the main contact platform for his social group. He walked around the house in his underwear, wrapped in a large soft blanket, for the entire duration of the lockdown, and most days since. On the other hand, our twelve year old son has thrived. He carries my large iPad in one hand and a Kindle in the other. He is more proficient at Zoom, Skype and every other communication platform than any other member of our household. He happily joined online classes, played Roblox and Minecraft with his friends, attended virtual soccer practice, and spent hours socializing with his friends and soccer teammates on Zoom. And of course, he has been taking online Mandarin classes.

Our oldest two were a freshman and a sophomore at a local public high school in our neighborhood when the pandemic started. Although it is not a particularly academically challenging school, they are both part of an academic academy and play varsity sports. Between the two of them, they had six teachers but only one — a history teacher — used Zoom, hosting two live classes or meetings with students each week. The other teachers were almost entirely absent. Their chemistry teacher sent an email to the students saying, "I don't do Zoom". She did not provide a single class instruction. The approach seems to have been that it is up to the teachers to determine how they teach remotely. This created a very uneven set of results and experiences for the students. When the district announced that students would be guaranteed not to receive a grade lower than the previous term's, most of my sons' friends simply gave up and phoned it in for the rest of the year.

From a parent perspective, it was an absolute disaster. It has been sad to see our children lose contact with their friends and classmates, while also seeing the absence of support from teachers. There was simply no interest in maintaining any level of academic curiosity in the students. And this is a point we have noticed almost universally across the schools we know. The priority seems to be on the interest of the teachers — who are undeniably carrying a heavy burden — but it comes at the expense of the students who are suffering as well.

The pandemic has exposed many cracks in the system. Perhaps these are cracks that would have gone unnoticed absent the pandemic. For instance, public schools in the United States are governed by School Districts, which have a superintendent and administrative staff who are answerable to a School Board. The members of the Board are volunteers who are usually elected to their Board positions, though in a majority of the cases, candidates run unopposed. For this reason, and because there are no requirements, nor compensation, Board members are largely unqualified. At times there are former teachers or principals, but usually it is a local parent who may actually view it as a potential stepping stone for the start of a political career. Despite their lack of expertise, these members hold significant influence over the lives of every public school student and family. That is glaringly apparent during the decision process on whether to reopen schools.

A few weeks ago, our School Board held an information meeting with five experts who were meant to advise the Board on reopenings. None of the experts were scientists. The closest thing was a local well-meaning pediatrician, with no expertise in virology or pandemics. The others were representatives of local wellness organizations, including mental health specialists.

But again, no applicable expertise that could guide the Board regarding the right decisions, protocols, or procedures to implement in connection with the opening of schools. So this is the problem: school district boards across the country, populated by well-meaning volunteer board members, use only local resources for expert input regarding the pandemic and its possible impact on school populations. Listening in on the meeting, it became very clear that the Board members had absolutely no idea what to consider when reopening schools and how to make a final decision. The safety of our children was in very uncertain hands.

The political divide in the United States is causing real damage to our children. Our President states that he wants schools to reopen, but gives no detailed guidelines, protocols, or scientific references. But with one tweet, the battle lines are drawn. Blue counties quickly announce they will be opening remotely, while conservative districts quickly announce that they will open schools in-person, without requiring masks. Parents are caught in the middle, the students are voiceless, and we are all left to listen to cable news or to read the news feeds that filter into our view.

In our community, we are going to open on August 24th on a remote learning basis. The universal opinion among the parents we know is that it was an unmitigated disaster in the spring, and there is no evidence that the schools are better prepared in the fall. No sports either. For a family that believes in the life lessons that are learned from team sports, it is sad to see our children miss their activities. For college bound juniors, the upcoming semesters are critical to showcase their talents to college coaches. Without competition, they have nothing to show. So without sports, and the poor distance learning experience, we as parents feel obligated to explore options for our children. Trust me, we understand how fortunate and privileged we are to be even in a position to consider alternatives. Many people around us are suffering true economic hardship and duress. We are focused on doing what we believe may be best for our children. They are depressed and have certainly lost some of their intellectual curiosity to learn. Thankfully, we have options, but not everyone does. The private schools we have visited have invested millions into Covid safety and preparation. These schools are a perfect example of organization, expertise, data collection, and analysis. They have developed protocols and processes, far exceeding those recommended by the CDC.

It is a major indictment of our total public school system that we find ourselves in the extremely stressful situation of considering spending our retirement funds to provide our children the chance of receiving a valuable education during this pandemic. We are considering uprooting our lives to avoid having them experience the public school remote learning experience again. Surely that must show you how bad we thought it was and how desperate we are. We do not blame anyone for the pandemic and we certainly understand that at the moment nobody can predict how long it will last. However, unless we collectively agree to fight the spread of the virus through masks, social distancing and rigorous testing, and if school districts are unwilling to put students first in designing and providing high quality remote learning, parents like us will be fleeing the system. But at the moment, we are still in the middle of the agonizing stage of deciding. Should we stay or should we go?

TR, University Student, Milan, Italy

I was among the first students affected by the virus, as I attend Bocconi University in Milan. When Bocconi announced they were closing their doors because of the virus, it felt like I was in a movie. Uncertain of how long I was leaving for, I packed a small suitcase and took the first flight home. What has affected me most throughout the pandemic was the loss of normalcy. The transition to online lectures and online exams was difficult, and the quality of teaching certainly went down. So did my ability to study. Suddenly, it became nearly impossible for me to complete a lecture a day.

Bocconi will be opening again in September to offer a mix of in-person and online lectures. We have a choice between continuing the next semester online or returning to the lecture halls. I am happy they decided to do so. I miss my student life, especially the freedom it offers. When the pandemic was in its earliest stages in Europe, I was infected with the virus. I was asymptomatic, so it did not affect me much.

Today, even though I am not worried for myself, I do have a few concerns. Bocconi is following the safety guidelines to the letter: markings on the floor, regular disinfection of high-touch surfaces, and filtered air in lecture halls. Still I worry that it is not enough. Bocconi has over 13,000 students with more than 100 different nationalities. While it is possible that other students will get infected and develop a severe case, it is professors who are most at risk. Many of my professors are older, which makes them more vulnerable to the virus.

I already know that the next academic year is going to be a weird one. I am not scared, but I am stressed by the possibility of the virus becoming uncontrollable again. I feel like the virus is taking away valuable experiences I should have, and while we are all trying to make the best of it, I don't want to go back to student life only to have it taken away from me again. I am putting a lot of hope into next semester—hope that all will go well. I now think back on my first semester fondly, even though it is always described as the worst semester at Bocconi.

I want to trust the right decisions are being made, but how can I when cases in Italy are back on the rise? Am I really expected to go back to the city that was once the epicenter of the pandemic in Europe just to attend lectures? Parties are such a big part of the Bocconi life, and where I met so many of my friends. How will we replace that? I know that I will have to make many adjustments to my life, but I do not know which ones yet. That is the part that scares me. I know that I am responsible and will do whatever it takes to keep myself and the people around me safe. I simply do not know how that will affect me mentally.

I believe that the first few months of the school year will be anxiety driven, and I worry that not everyone will have a support system strong enough to get them through it. GPAs, including my own, have gone down. That took a toll on me, and definitely affected my motivation to do well on the exams that followed. I hope that returning to in-person lectures will motivate me again, but I also hope that Bocconi will provide the necessary support for students to succeed.

Overall, I am mostly feeling uncertain. I want to believe that I will be able to go back to normalcy, or something close to it, but I have very few reasons to believe that current attempts to do so will work. I am torn between pessimism and optimism. One might be closer to reality while the other might be better for my own mentality.

FT, Mother of Three High School and University Students

Being a mother of three children, ages 19, 16 and 12, I wish my children could go back to school without restrictions as soon as possible.

My attitude toward Covid-19 has not ceased to evolve since the beginning of the pandemic. At first, I believed it would not affect our family. Covid-19, as most disasters in the world, was only on the news for me.

Then I started to educate myself and read all I could find on the virus, from the media to people around us who were knowledgeable on the subject. The virus became part of our daily lives, but I still did not feel directly threatened by it, as it was said that only people with underlying health conditions were at risk and that most people could be healed.

Very quickly, however, it became clear that the health workforce was not prepared to cope with a massive outbreak of the virus. The entire medical infrastructure would collapse unless we all decided to help protect the most fragile among us, adopt a responsible attitude, and actively contribute to stopping the spread of the virus. By protecting others, we were protecting ourselves.

On March 13th, a Friday afternoon, the Minister of Education announced that all public schools would close the following Monday until further notice. Deans had to improvise, organize, and communicate with staff, students and parents. They were struggling to put in place online teaching that would allow children to continue learning from home, keep in touch with teachers and classmates, and complete their education on time.

Surprisingly, the system worked quite well. My children turned out to be very disciplined and managed to stay connected with the school. They all finished their year. Schools partially opened again three weeks before summer break, which was very important for children as they could say goodbye to their classmates and teachers for the summer and look forward to a "normal" return to schools.

This isn't the case everywhere, it seems. Most universities have already announced their intention to keep online teaching at least partially in place. The reasons for this are not only sanitary but also economical. Are the best interests of our children still a priority?

Online teaching and the distance it creates between students and teachers will oblige our children to be more disciplined and responsible about their education on their own. I admire them for their ability to adapt and cope. They are truly learning to take responsibility for themselves, take charge, and make the best out of the situation that has been imposed on them.

This will, however, never replace the benefit of going physically to school—to play and learn, to be part of a community, and to debate and exchange ideas with teachers and classmates in a classroom the way we did. I do hope they will soon be given the freedom to resume the normal path to education once again. I am quite confident in the future, as this shall pass.

Sejal Mistry, Mother of Two Grade School Students

Like most parents, I have been overwhelmed and frustrated to have my children with me every single hour of every single day. I tried to maintain the same level of pre-Covid productivity and efficiency at work and at home, but viruses—like children—do not care about schedules.

Like a toddler bent on sowing chaos, Covid upended our lives in March and April, when Singapore imposed restrictions and eventually went into lockdown. I count myself and my family lucky to be situated where we are in the new global order. Small countries, like Singapore, have shown calm, rational leadership, while larger countries like the United States have flailed. Singapore controlled the epidemic exceptionally well in its early days, until a latent local epidemic in migrant worker communities later caught the country unawares and spiked the national case count considerably.

On April 7, Singapore entered into lockdown. This was locally referred to as a "circuit breaker" period, aptly evoking the image of halting an electrical current. It planned for a three-phase

Covid response—the circuit breaker period of lockdown (Phase 1) followed by an easing of restrictions (Phases 2 & 3). We did not know when we would enter the next phase, only that it would be triggered when the government gained enough confidence that community transmission was on the decline.

Under circuit breaker, everyone had to stay at home except for occasional excursions for essentials: groceries and doctor's visits. All social gatherings with members outside your household were not allowed—not even within your home. And this certainly meant that all schools were shuttered, too. So began our days, weeks behind the rest of the world, of Zoom calls, virtual spelling tests, and math workbooks.

In early June, when spread of the virus had slowed, Singapore exited circuit breaker and entered Phase 2. Schools were reopened and we all breathed a collective sigh of relief (while masked of course). All public places, schools included, now had to enforce a series of measures to keep rates of community transmission low: 1) safe distancing of at least six feet apart, 2) mandatory wearing of masks, except when dining/drinking, 3) registering yourself through a QR code in every business or public place you enter, and 4) no gatherings larger than five. Students were allowed to return to their classrooms in groups greater than five, but strict measures of distancing and hygiene were enforced.

School days under Covid lasted only a few weeks. My kids are now on summer holidays until September, and most will return in August. But those few weeks were instructive, as I got a glimpse of how schools and the local government are taking measures to ensure the protection of children, faculty, and their communities.

I plan to send my kids to school in September because I trust the government's assessment and control of Covid spread in Singapore. We have not entered Phase 3 and the government also has stated that it does not know when Phase 3 will begin. The successful arrival of this phase, during which all remaining restrictions will lift, depends on our current adherence to government-mandated rules around social distancing and masks, which in turn are reflections of the rules of virus transmission and public health. While we are well on our way to Phase 3, I know that we can quickly revert to a Phase 1 lockdown if the virus takes hold again.

The decisions of when my kids go back to school are essentially made by the virus and interpreted locally by experts and officials. While I may not agree with all the decisions, I understand that they are made in an environment of imperfect information. These are decisions I trust.

Acknowledgements

I would first like to thank the students, parents and grandparents who shared their thoughts and concerns with me throughout the writing of this book, especially those who were generous enough to share their stories within the book itself.

To my children, stepchildren and grandchildren — Mara, Alexander, Karina, Manuela, Camila, Pedro Agustin, Enrique Matias, and Carlos Eduardo — I would like to thank each of you for the lessons you teach me each day about resilience, responsibility, and loving kindness. Above all, I would like to thank my wife, Maria Eugenia, for her love, patience, and tireless efforts to care for us all.

William A. Haseltine, PhD

I would also like to extend my thanks to Brian Stauffer, who designed the cover of this book and my companion book, *A Family Guide to Covid.* Finally, to my colleagues at ACCESS Health International, I would like to extend my deepest thanks, especially to Shreya Kavuru, Tess Reckinger, Jo Gurch, and Anna Dirksen for their research and editorial support throughout the writing of this book.

APPENDIX

Summary of School Mitigation Strategies

Strategy	Role in limiting transmission	Considerations for implementation
Wearing masks (surgical, fabric)	The virus is spread through respiratory droplets from breathing, talking, coughing, and sneezing. The mask catches the droplets before they can spread.	Requiring masks for all students and staff is most effective.
Hand-washing	Droplets containing the virus can spread to hands from coughing, sneezing or from surfaces. If a person then touches their mouth, nose, or eyes they may become infected. Hand-washing removes the virus.	Soap and water is most effective. Hand-sanitizer is appropriate to use if soap and water are not available. Minimum times for hand washing – before and after eating, after using the restroom.

Physical distancing – Maintaining 3 to 6 feet between students and staff	When people are in close contact they can easily breathe in droplets containing the virus that other people have exhaled. Most droplets will fall to the ground within 3-6 feet of being exhaled.	How this is implemented will depend on the number of students in the school and the size of classrooms. The key is maintaining sufficient space between students and between students and the teacher. There is no evidence about the relative effectiveness of different ways of implementing physical distancing in schools.
Eliminating large gatherings	If a person is sick, large gatherings with close contact mean that many other people may be infected.	This includes eliminating assemblies, large sports events, and large numbers of students in common areas (cafeteria, hallways, entryways)
Creating cohorts (one teacher stays with the same group of students)	Smaller groups of students in a classroom allow for more distance between people. In addition, limiting contact with many other people,	Members of the cohort do not mix with the rest of the school. The teacher should also have minimal contact with students and other

	cuts down on possible exposures.	staff outside of the cohort.
Cleaning	Droplets can land on surfaces and remain active for 1-3 days. If a person touches the surface with their hands and then touches their mouth, nose or eyes, they can contract the virus.	Regular cleaning is important to eliminate the virus on surfaces. Routine cleaning with appropriate disinfectant is sufficient. Cleaning is particularly important for high touch areas and shared materials.
Ventilation	While most droplets containing the virus fall out of the air, some can stay suspended. If enough suspended droplets accumulate they could be breathed in by occupants. When fresh air is added to a room where virus is present, the amount of virus is diluted or eliminated.	Small rooms with poor ventilation are likely to increase risk of transmission. Open windows and doors to increase circulation of outdoor air as much as possible. Moving classroom activities out-of-doors is also an option for improving ventilation.

| Air filtering | Mechanical heating, cooling and ventilation control and regulate the amount and quality of air in buildings for humidity, temperature and particulates. For efficiency, some systems recirculate the indoor air as much as possible to reduce the energy costs of treating outside air. If there are droplets containing the virus in the air, recirculation could spread Covid within a building. Upgraded filters can remove droplets containing the virus from the air. | To provide maximum protection, upgrade the filters used in the HVAC system, increase the fresh air intake, and increase the level of humidity. |

| Temperature and symptom screening | The intent is to identify individuals who have Covid-19 and prevent them from bringing the virus into the building. | There is increasing evidence that people are contagious before they show symptoms. This means the considerable time and costs to screen all students before entering buses or schools may be of limited value for identifying Covid cases. Studies in airports show limited value. However, parents should know the symptoms for Covid-19 and screen their children and household for them cach day before sending children to school. |

Table 4. School mitigation strategies

Source: National Academies of Sciences, Engineering, and Medicine

WHAT WILL IT COST TO REOPEN SCHOOLS?

This document estimates some of the expenses school districts may incur in response to the COVID-19 pandemic and as they plan to reopen for the 2020–2021 school year. These calculations assume the statistics of an average* school district with 3,659 students, 8 school buildings, 183 classrooms, 329 staff members, and 40 school buses (transporting at 25% capacity, or 915 students, to comply with recommended social distancing guidelines).

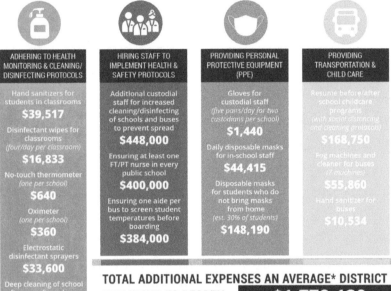

ADHERING TO HEALTH MONITORING & CLEANING/ DISINFECTING PROTOCOLS

Hand sanitizers for students in classrooms
$39,517

Disinfectant wipes for classrooms
(four/day per classroom)
$16,833

No-touch thermometer
(one per school)
$640

Oximeter
(one per school)
$360

Electrostatic disinfectant sprayers
$33,600

Deep cleaning of school after a confirmed case
$26,000

HIRING STAFF TO IMPLEMENT HEALTH & SAFETY PROTOCOLS

Additional custodial staff for increased cleaning/disinfecting of schools and buses to prevent spread
$448,000

Ensuring at least one FT/PT nurse in every public school
$400,000

Ensuring one aide per bus to screen student temperatures before boarding
$384,000

PROVIDING PERSONAL PROTECTIVE EQUIPMENT (PPE)

Gloves for custodial staff
(five pairs/day for two custodians per school)
$1,440

Daily disposable masks for in-school staff
$44,415

Disposable masks for students who do not bring masks from home
(est. 30% of students)
$148,190

PROVIDING TRANSPORTATION & CHILD CARE

Resume before/after school childcare programs
(with social distancing and cleaning protocols)
$168,750

Fog machines and cleaner for buses
(7 machines)
$55,860

Hand sanitizer for buses
$10,534

TOTAL ADDITIONAL EXPENSES AN AVERAGE* DISTRICT MAY INCUR TO REOPEN: **$1,778,139**

*Costs will vary by district depending on many factors, including regional/market price as economy of scale (i.e., larger districts may have access to lower unit costs because they can buy in higher volumes), and the availability of labor and goods necessary to comply with recommended social distancing and cleaning protocols. Model assumes 25% transportation capacity to adhere to social distancing guidelines. (Bus fleets would need to quadruple in size to safely transport 100% of students under COVID-19 circumstances, which is financially unfeasible for districts.)

This list of costs is not intended to be exhaustive but illustrates how the overall cost of school operations will substantially increase to safely reopen as a direct result of the COVID-19 pandemic. For more information on the impact of the COVID-19 pandemic on K–12 education, please contact ASBO International & AASA.

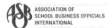

External References:
"Now What? Navigating K-12 Reopening, A Collaborative Planning Process?" National Council on School Facilities. Working Document, May 2020.
"School Bus Driver Pay Rises as Shortage Worsens," Thomas McMahon, *School Bus Fleet Magazine*, November 2018.
"Total School Districts. Student Enrollment by State and Metro Area," Governing The Future of States and Localities, eRepublic. Accessed June 2020.

[i] Long, Quan-Xin, et al. "Clinical and Immunological Assessment of Asymptomatic SARS-CoV-2 Infections." Nature Medicine, 2020, doi:10.1038/s41591-020-0965-6.

[ii] Means, Mary L., and James F. Voss. "Who Reasons Well? Two Studies of Informal Reasoning Among Children of Different Grade, Ability, and Knowledge Levels." Cognition and Instruction, vol. 14, no. 2, 1996, pp. 139–78. *Crossref*, doi:10.1207/s1532690xci1402_1.

[iii] Moffitt, Terrie E., et al. "A Gradient of Childhood Self-Control Predicts Health, Wealth, and Public Safety." *Proceedings of the National Academy of Sciences*, vol. 108, no. 7, 2011, pp. 2693–98. *Crossref*, doi:10.1073/pnas.1010076108.

[iv] Stern, Alexandra M., et al. "Closing The Schools: Lessons From The 1918–19 U.S. Influenza Pandemic." Health Affairs, vol. 28, no. Supplement 1, 2009, pp. w1066–78. *Crossref*, doi:10.1377/hlthaff.28.6.w1066.

[v] Ferguson, Neil M., et al. "Strategies for Mitigating an Influenza Pandemic." *Nature*, vol. 442, no. 7101,

2006, pp. 448–52. *Crossref*, doi:10.1038/nature04795.

vi "June Member Survey: The Burden Is Real - Immediate Action Needed to Support and Retain Working Parents." Cleo, 2020. hicleo.com/blog/the-burden-is-real-immediate-action-needed-to-support-and-retain-working-parents/.

vii Calderon, Valerie J. "U.S. Parents Say COVID-19 Harming Child's Mental Health." Gallup.com, Gallup, 17 July 2020, news.gallup.com/poll/312605/parents-say-covid-harming-child-mental-health.aspx.

viii Pollan, Marina, et al. "A Population-Based Seroepidemiological Study of SARS-CoV-2 in Spain (ENE-COVID)." *SSRN Electronic Journal*, 2020, doi:10.2139/ssrn.3616010.

ix Havers, Fiona P., et al. "Seroprevalence of Antibodies to SARS-CoV-2 in Six Sites in the United States, March 23-May 3, 2020." 2020, doi:10.1101/2020.06.25.20140384.

x Rees, Eleanor M., et al. "COVID-19 Length of Hospital Stay: A Systematic Review and Data

Synthesis." *MedRxiv*, 2020. *Crossref*,
doi:10.1101/2020.04.30.20084780.

[xi] Davies, Nicholas G., et al. "Age-Dependent Effects
in the Transmission and Control of COVID-19
Epidemics." *Nature Medicine*, 2020. *Crossref*,
doi:10.1038/s41591-020-0962-9.

[xii] CDC Covid-19 Response Team. "Coronavirus
Disease 2019 in Children — United States, February
12-April 2, 2020." *Centers for Disease Control and
Prevention*, 10 Apr. 2020,
www.cdc.gov/mmwr/volumes/69/wr/mm6914e4.htm.

[xiii] Fateh-Moghadam, Pirous, et al. "Contact Tracing
during Phase I of the COVID-19 Pandemic in the
Province of Trento, Italy: Key Findings and
Recommendations." 2020,
doi:10.1101/2020.07.16.20127357.

[xiv] Abdel-Mannan, Omar, et al. "Neurologic and
Radiographic Findings Associated With COVID-19
Infection in Children." *JAMA Neurology*, 2020.
Crossref, doi:10.1001/jamaneurol.2020.2687.

[xv] Rae, Matthew, et al. "Millions of Seniors Live In
Households with School-Age Children." KFF, 16 July

2020, www.kff.org/coronavirus-covid-19/issue-brief/millions-of-seniors-live-in-households-with-school-age-children/?utm_campaign=KFF-2020-Coronavirus&utm_medium=email&_hsenc=p2ANqtz-9kd5S9chlVN0ee-R2WiQIN8uvti4sdAdGM2aU_Fg98apt3DgM8Q_mNOr7MJhkiYm0PIMeUWvYcPF3AKAeOxbhCuMclXO2WcBt12O4WHFPMLFxDWQY&_hsmi=91498223&utm_content=91498223&utm_source=hs_email&hsCtaTracking=b8ca7c12-25ad-4e6d-b473-6af6f90d6992%7C1a007d8b-55ac-4b52-ab1a-39f05b0caaba.

xvi Guthrie, Brandon L., et al. Washington State Department of Health/UW Metacenter for Pandemic Preparedness/START Center, 2020, *Summary of School Re-Opening Models and Implementation Approaches During the COVID 19 Pandemic*, globalhealth.washington.edu/sites/default/files/COVID-19%20Schools%20Summary%20%282%29.pdf?mkt_tok=eyJpljoiTkRreE5XWXlORFF3TXppNeCIslnQiOiJIbVNQTTVySEo0Vzk1cHVBZVVqWnFFGVmR1UEJxRGdpd01mTXg4OGw3Mk5nTnpppmaUoyMGt2UXlwWVVZBOE5GVjlybHA5aStrbzJ3MUxsanoxamZibml

ocmpSbXZyVFVoV0VHYU1aTGx0RnpsMXlmOEtX
SVJqaDJsZ0RJU1BQcVZjZSJ9.

[xvii] Couzin-Frankel, Jennifer, et al. "School Openings across Globe Suggest Ways to Keep Coronavirus at Bay, despite Outbreaks." *Science*, 7 July 2020, doi:10.1126/science.abd7107.

[xviii] Vegas, Emiliana. "Reopening the World: Reopening Schools—Insights from Denmark and Finland." *Brookings*, 6 July 2020, www.brookings.edu/blog/education-plus-development/2020/07/06/reopening-the-world-reopening-schools-insights-from-denmark-and-finland.

[xix] Couzin-Frankel, Jennifer, et al. "School Openings across Globe Suggest Ways to Keep Coronavirus at Bay, despite Outbreaks." *Science*, 7 July 2020, doi:10.1126/science.abd7107.

[xx] Denyer, Simon. "In a Tokyo School, Temperature Checks and Silent Lunches as Japan Restarts Classes." The Washington Post, WP Company, 7 June 2020, www.washingtonpost.com/world/asia_pacific/japan-

coronavirus-schools-reopen/2020/06/06/9047be8c-a645-11ea-8681-7d471bf20207_story.html.

[xxi] Schwartz , Felicia, and Dov Lieber. "Israelis Fear Schools Reopened Too Soon as Covid-19 Cases Climb." *Wall Street Journal*, 14 July 2020, www.wsj.com/articles/israelis-fear-schools-reopened-too-soon-as-covid-19-cases-climb-11594760001.

[xxii] Harvard T.H. Chan School of Public Health. "How School Buildings Influence Student Health, Thinking and Performance." *Schools For Health*, For Health, schools.forhealth.org/.

[xxiii] Xie, Xinyan, et al. "Mental Health Status Among Children in Home Confinement During the Coronavirus Disease 2019 Outbreak in Hubei Province, China." *JAMA Pediatrics*, 2020. *Crossref*, doi:10.1001/jamapediatrics.2020.1619.

[xxiv] Jones, Carolyn. "Student Anxiety, Depression Increasing during School Closures, Survey Finds." EdSource, 13 May 2020, edsource.org/2020/student-anxiety-depression-increasing-during-school-closures-survey-finds/631224.

xxv Cirbus, Amy. "How to Manage Homeschooling During COVID-19." *Talkspace*, 16 Apr. 2020, www.talkspace.com/blog/coronavirus-homeschooling-home-school-tips-parenting.

xxvi Nye, Author: Rich. "Greenfield-Central Student Tests Positive for COVID-19 on First Day Back to School." Wthr.com, 31 July 2020, www.wthr.com/article/news/health/coronavirus/greenfield-central-schools-begin-in-person-classes-anticipating-eventual-coronavirus-case/531-e1b7e9f2-f36d-468d-9ab2-2139a1b1e4f6.

CPSIA information can be obtained
at www.ICGtesting.com
Printed in the USA
BVHW021252120820
586232BV00016B/385

9 780578 743615